SPORTING SKILLS

NETBALL

CLIVE GIFFORD

Published in 2013 by Wayland

Copyright © Wayland 2013

Wayland
Hachette Children's Books
338 Euston Road
London NW1 3BH

Wayland Australia
Level 17/207 Kent Street
Sydney, NSW 2000

Editorial Director: Rasha Elsaeed

Produced by Tall Tree Ltd
Editor: Jon Richards
Designer: Ben Ruocco
Photographer: Michael Wicks
Consultant: Susannah Oates

British Library Cataloguing in Publication Data

Gifford, Clive.
  Netball. -- (Sporting skills)
  1. Netball--Juvenile literature.
  I. Title II. Series
  796.3'24-dc22

ISBN: 9780750278652

10 9 8 7 6 5 4 3 2 1

Printed in China

Wayland is a division of Hachette Children's
Books, an Hachette UK company.
www.hachette.co.uk

Picture credits
All photographs taken by Michael Wicks,
except:
Front cover Dreasmtime.com/Koh Sze Kiat
and Dreamstime.com/ Steven Pike,
5 br Dreamstime.com/Shariff Che' Lah

Acknowledgements
The author and publisher would like to thank
the following people for their help and
participation in this book:
The girls from Maiden Erlegh School

The website addresses (URLs) included in this
book were valid at the time of going to press.
However, because of the nature of the
Internet, it is possible that some addresses
may have changed, or sites may have changed
or closed down since publication. While the
author and Publisher regret any inconvenience
this may cause the readers, no responsibility
for any such changes can be accepted by
either the author or the Publisher.

Disclaimer
In prepara... .... due to the
been exer... ....
activities ... .ues depict...d. The
publishers ... .t that they can accept no
liability fo... ...any loss or injury sustained...
When lear... ....
to get exp... .... follow a
manufactu...er's instructions.

In this b... ....have used different
coloured arrows to show the movement of
the ball and different body parts. A blue
arrow indicates the ball movement, a red
arrow shows body movement, while a
yellow arrow shows the movement of a
body part, such as the arms.

CONTENTS

WHAT IS NETBALL?

Netball is a team sport played by millions all over the world. A game lasts one hour and is split up into four quarters. Two teams, each with seven players (with up to five substitutes on the bench), aim to move the ball into a position to shoot it into a net to score a goal.

WORLDWIDE APPEAL

Netball is played in more than 70 countries around the world. In New Zealand and Australia, an exciting new competition, the ANZ Championship, started in 2008, with top players paid to play in the ten-team league whose games are watched by large crowds. Major sports competitions, such as the Asian Games and the Commonwealth Games, feature netball and the World Championships are held once every four years. In the UK, the nine-team Netball Superleague (NSL) is the top level of club competition.

Netball history

Netball is similar to basketball but without dribbling (running with the ball as it is bounced up and down). In fact, the inventor of netball, an American woman called Clara Baer, asked the inventor of basketball for a copy of his rules, and from this she wrote the first full set of netball rules in 1901. Twenty-three years later, New Zealand was the first country to have a national association for netball, while the World Championships was first held in 1963. Today, the International Netball Federation runs netball around the world.

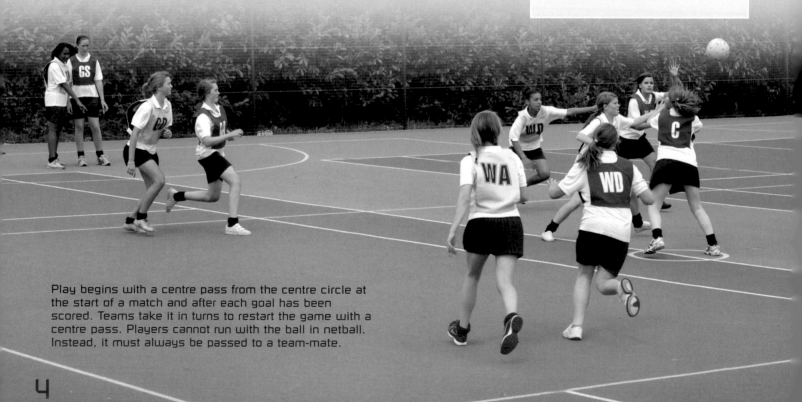

Play begins with a centre pass from the centre circle at the start of a match and after each goal has been scored. Teams take it in turns to restart the game with a centre pass. Players cannot run with the ball in netball. Instead, it must always be passed to a team-mate.

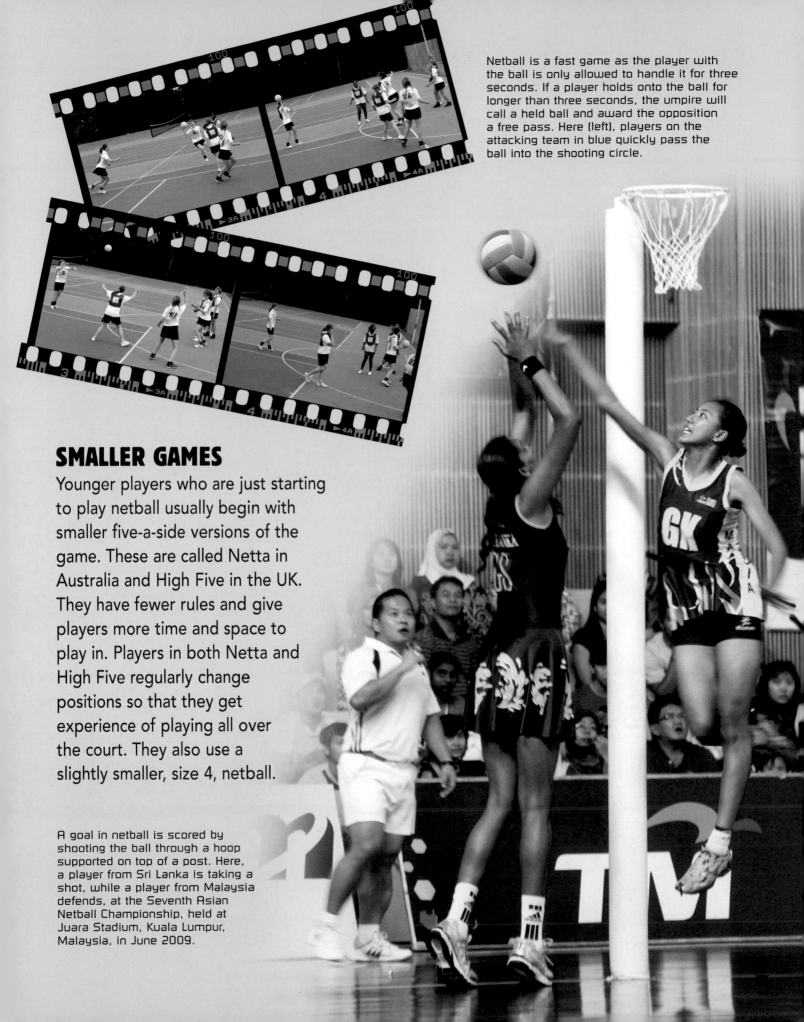

Netball is a fast game as the player with the ball is only allowed to handle it for three seconds. If a player holds onto the ball for longer than three seconds, the umpire will call a held ball and award the opposition a free pass. Here (left), players on the attacking team in blue quickly pass the ball into the shooting circle.

SMALLER GAMES

Younger players who are just starting to play netball usually begin with smaller five-a-side versions of the game. These are called Netta in Australia and High Five in the UK. They have fewer rules and give players more time and space to play in. Players in both Netta and High Five regularly change positions so that they get experience of playing all over the court. They also use a slightly smaller, size 4, netball.

A goal in netball is scored by shooting the ball through a hoop supported on top of a post. Here, a player from Sri Lanka is taking a shot, while a player from Malaysia defends, at the Seventh Asian Netball Championship, held at Juara Stadium, Kuala Lumpur, Malaysia, in June 2009.

THE NETBALL COURT

Netball can be played both outdoors and indoors. Top competitions, however, are always played on indoor courts. The netball court is 30.5 metres (100 feet) long and 15.25 metres (50 feet) wide. It has a simple set of markings and a goal post at each end. Each goal post is 3.05 metres (10 feet) tall.

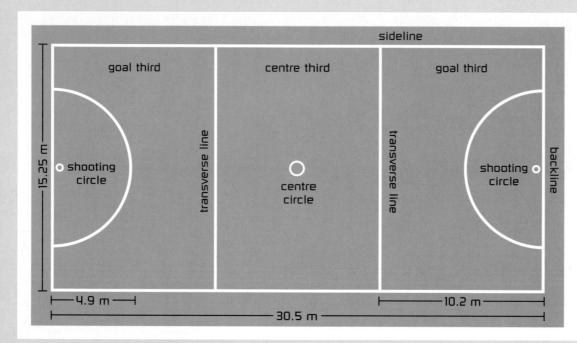

The court
The lines marking out the court should be no more than 5 centimetres (2 inches) wide. Unlike basketball, the posts at either end do not have a backboard against which players can bounce the ball.

COURT MARKINGS

In the middle of a netball court is the small centre circle, which measures 0.9 metres (3 feet) across. The court is split into three equal areas by two lines called transverse lines. At each end of the court is a large semi-circle known as the shooting circle. Goals can only be scored by shots taken from inside the shooting circle. The edge of the court is marked by the sidelines and backlines. If the ball goes out over a sideline, the team that did not touch it last restarts the game with a throw-in (see page 7).

DID YOU KNOW?
The first netball nets were not open at the bottom. This meant that players and officials had to climb to the top of the post to retrieve the ball when a goal was scored.

A full-sized netball, size 5, is about the same size as a soccer ball but has a rough outer surface to help players grip the ball. Check it is inflated correctly before playing a game or training.

The ring at the top of each goal post is 38 centimetres (15 inches) wide and supported 15 centimetres (6 inches) in front of the post.

This centre (above) has stepped over the sideline with her right foot while catching the ball. The ball is out of play when the player holding it steps over a sideline or the ball bounces outside the court.

Restarts

When the ball goes out of play over a baseline, a restart takes place from under one of the posts (left).

If the ball goes out of play over a sideline, then play restarts with a throw-in from where it crossed the line (left).

Netball is a fast-paced game that requires a great deal of jumping, stretching and bending. As such, players should make sure that they are properly warmed up before starting to play to avoid any injuries.

THE RIGHT KIT

Netball players should wear loose-fitting kit to allow for plenty of movement during a match. Boys wear shorts and a t-shirt, while girls wear an all-in-one netball dress or a skirt and netball top. Players have letters on the fronts and backs of their shirts or on bibs. These letters refer to playing positions and tell referees where the players should be on the court (see page 9). Wearing suitable shoes and socks is very important. Thick cotton sports socks will help cushion your feet and stop you getting blisters. Netball trainers should be light in weight but offer plenty of protection and support for your feet. They should also provide the right amount of grip on the court. Make sure your fingernails are trimmed and do not wear jewellery when training or playing matches.

This player is ready for her game wearing a sports skirt, vest, socks and training shoes. She has put on a positional bib to show that she is playing Wing Attack (WA).

Player positions

The seven players on a team each play in a particular position, such as Wing Attack (WA), Wing Defence (WD) or Centre (C). Goal Attack (GA) and Goal Shooter (GS) are the only players on a team allowed inside the shooting circle to score goals. At the other end of the court, Goal Defence (GD) and the Goalkeeper (GK) are the only two team members allowed inside the shooting circle that their team is defending. They try to stop attacks from opposing teams. The thirds of the court and the two shooting circles make up the five playing zones. Each player is allowed only into certain playing zones, depending on their position (see below). When players move into zones they are not allowed in, one of the umpires will signal offside. This sees the opposing team awarded a free pass.

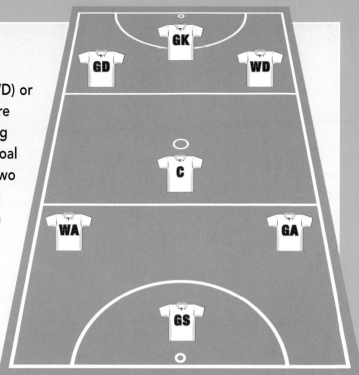

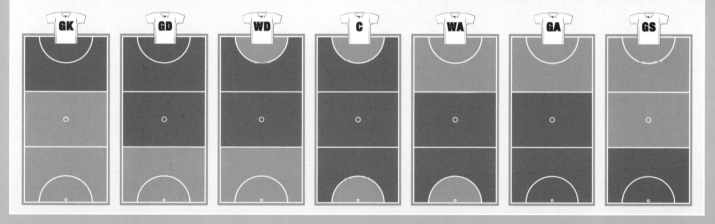

GETTING READY TO PLAY

A warm-up can start with some gentle jogging (right, above). This will raise your heart rate and increase the flow of blood to your muscles. This can then be followed by a series of stretches to your body's joints and muscles, from your neck down to your ankles. The girls shown here (right, below) are stretching the muscles of their upper legs, under the guidance of a coach.

THE UMPIRE AND RULES

A game of netball is run by two officials called umpires. These officials enforce the sport's rules, which are designed to make the game fast, flowing and free from contact or fouls.

THE OFFICIALS

The umpires each take charge of half of the court and start and stop a game with a whistle blow. They must rule on whether the ball has left the court and which team should be awarded the throw-in (see page 7), as well as ensuring that players stay in their allowed playing areas. The umpires must also decide whether rules have been broken, such as a player holding onto the ball for too long or taking steps while in possession of the ball. If any of these events occur, the other team will be awarded a free pass. Top-level games also feature a timekeeper to keep track of how long has been played and a scorer to record how many points have been scored.

(see page 7)

The player with the red bib is committing a foul by using the ball to push the defending player with the blue bib. In this instance, the umpire would stop play and award a free pass to the team with the blue bibs.

This umpire is showing two netball signals. On the left she is indicating that a foul has occurred. On the right she holds her arm straight ahead to show that a goal has been scored and play should restart from the centre circle.

PENALTY PASSES

Netball is a non-contact sport, so pushing, pulling an opponent's clothes, barging and tripping an opponent are all illegal. If one of these serious offences occurs, then the umpire will award a penalty pass (see right). If an attacking player is fouled inside the shooting circle, then she can either pass or take a shot at the goal. If a player repeatedly fouls, then the umpire can send her off, forcing her team to continue with one player fewer.

If two players catch the ball at the same time, an umpire will award a toss-up. In a toss-up, the two players stand on either side of the umpire, who then throws the ball up for the players to jump and catch.

Penalty pass

1 Here the defender is standing less than 0.9 metres (3 feet) from the attacker. An umpire will award a penalty pass.

2 The defender must move out of the way of the attacker and stand next to her, alllowing the attacker to make an unchallenged pass to a team-mate.

3 Once the penalty pass has been made, both the attacker and defender can then continue as before.

SHORT PASSING

Passing moves the ball around the court from player to player. Short passes, such as the chest pass or bounce pass, are the safest type of pass, because they are harder for opposition players to intercept.

CHEST AND BOUNCE PASSES

The chest pass can be accurate and effective over short distances and can be made quickly, because it is usually the place where the receiver catches the ball. To make a chest pass, the hands are placed behind and to the side of the ball. The arms are then thrust forwards in the direction of the intended pass. Sometimes, an opponent who is marking very closely makes a straight chest pass impossible. To get the ball past the marker, some players may play a short bounce pass, throwing the ball down to the side of and behind the marker so that it bounces up and into the receiver's hands. The bounce pass can be made with either one hand or two.

When viewed from the front, you can see that this player has followed through correctly, pushing her arms out towards her intended target so that the pass is accurate.

Chest pass

1 To make a chest pass, the hands should hold the ball with the fingers pointing inwards, towards each other. Both the forearms and the upper arms are then pushed forwards.

2 The wrists are flicked forwards to add extra power to the pass. The player follows through by extending her arms in the direction of the pass after the ball has been released.

1 Here, the defender in blue is blocking a direct pass between the two attackers, but has left room for a low bounce pass.

2 The attacker in red uses a chest pass to push the ball down past the defender so that it bounces off the ground. The attacker has to judge where to bounce the ball carefully.

3 A successful bounce pass sees the ball bounce up into the hands of the receiving attacker at about waist height, making the catch as easy as possible.

TIMING AND ACCURACY

For any pass to be successful, it needs to be thrown with accuracy and the right amount of force. A weak pass may give a player from the other team the chance to intercept it, while too strong a pass can make the ball overshoot the intended target and go out of play. Improving your passing speed and accuracy comes with practice. This can be in training or in casual practice with one or two team-mates. Alternatively, you can practise on your own by simply throwing a ball against a wall.

Here, three players are practising their passing in a triangle. This allows them to make a series of quick passes to improve their co-ordination.

13

RECEIVING THE BALL

Receiving the ball is more than just about catching it. Players also have to be aware of important rules regarding footwork and handling of the ball.

CATCHING

As soon as you are in space, call or signal for a pass, move to receive it and keep your eyes on the ball. You want to try to watch the ball right into your hands, as some passes can dip slightly as they arrive or the ball may deflect off another player on its way to you. The simplest form of catch uses both hands held in a 'W' shape with the ball ideally caught between waist and chest height. On many occasions the ball will fly to you at a height or angle where using two hands is not possible. In these situations, you can touch the ball once in the air, tapping or slapping it towards you so that you can get your other hand on it as soon as possible. You are not allowed to make a fist to punch the ball or tap it more than once.

This player has put her hands together so that she is ready to receive the ball, making a 'W' shape with her thumbs and fingers.

Catching

1 This player is ready to receive a pass. She has put her hands in a 'W' shape (see above) and is holding her arms out.

2 As the ball arrives, she wraps her fingers around the ball and pulls her arms in to cushion the ball's arrival and slow it down.

3 She brings the ball into her chest and squats slightly to further absorb some of the ball's speed.

Being able to jump and catch a high ball is a useful skill as it can give you an advantage over defending players.

THE FOOTWORK RULE

If you catch the ball in the air, the first foot that touches the ground is called your landing foot. You can either keep this foot still and turn, or pivot, about it (see right), or you can take a step with your other foot and lift your landing foot. However, you must pass the ball before your landing foot touches the ground again. If you do not, then the umpire will signal that you have broken the stepping rule and award a free pass to the other team. If you receive the ball with both feet on the ground, the footwork rule still applies but you can choose which foot is your landing foot.

Catching drills

These players are practising catching. The player on the left is throwing the ball at different heights so that the catching player can practise taking chest-high passes, low passes and high passes that force her to jump.

Catch and pivot

1 Here, the attacker in red is catching a high pass, while the player in blue moves in to defend and block a pass.

2 The attacker has landed on her right foot (her landing foot) and is pivoting away from the defender using her left foot.

3 The attacker has now pivoted away from the defender and can make a pass without the defender blocking it.

AdVANCed PASSING

The bounce pass and the chest pass are just two of a wide range of passes that netball players can use. Mastering different passes will make moving the ball around the court faster, easier and much more accurate.

Overhead pass

1 With the ball held in two hands behind the head, the player moves her weight onto her front foot.

2 As she moves her weight forwards, she brings her hands in an arc over the top of her head and releases the ball in the direction of her target.

LONGER PASSING

Longer passing can be ideal to start a fast break when one team has intercepted the ball and finds one of its attackers free and in space. They can also be used to switch play from one side of the court to another or when a passer is under pressure from a marker and cannot make an easy, short pass. There are two main ways of passing the ball longer distances – the overhead pass and the shoulder pass. However, the pass cannot be too long as this could result in an over-a-third penalty being awarded (see page 17).

3 Once she has released the ball, the player follows through with her arms in the direction of the target. This helps to make the pass as accurate as possible.

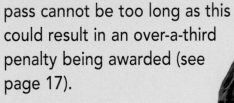
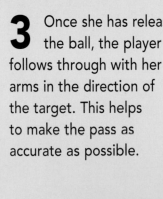

1 To make a shoulder pass, the ball is held in one hand. As the player moves her weight forwards, she brings her throwing arm over her shoulder.

2 At the right moment, the player releases the ball towards the target and follows through with the passing arm.

FAKES AND FLIPS

When an opposing player is defending closely, it is sometimes possible to pretend or fake to make one type of pass, then as the defender leans or moves to cover that pass, quickly change to make a different pass. For example, an attacker can lean low as if to make a bounce pass. As the defender lowers her arms and body to cover that move, the passer can spring upwards and release a quick overhead pass. Another way of passing the ball around defenders is the flip pass. This is a short, soft pass, flicked with the wrists and fingers underarm by the passer.

DID YOU KNOW?

At the 2003 World Championships, New Zealand thrashed the Cook Islands 107–18. New Zealand went on to win the championship for the first time in 16 years.

1 Long passes cannot break the over-a-third rule. This is where a player's pass crosses both of the transverse lines that cross the court. Here (above), the Goal Defence in blue has spotted a Wing Attack team-mate in space and has launched a long pass from her own defending third.

2 The Wing Attack has caught the pass, but she is standing in the attacking third of the court. The pass has crossed both of the transverse lines, breaking the over-a-third rule. The umpire will stop play and award a free throw to the defending team in red.

Over-a-third rule

EVASION SKILLS

There are a number of ways to get away from an opponent marking you so that you can receive the ball. The simplest way involves simply sprinting away from a defender. A lot of the time, however, outwitting a marker calls for more trickery.

DID YOU KNOW?

New Zealand was the last nation to call the sport netball. Up until 1970, the sport was known as 'women's basketball'.

Faking

1 To fake a move, the attacker in red begins by taking a step to her right. To help make the fake convincing, she may drop her right shoulder to exaggerate the move.

2 The defender in blue sees the attacker move and starts to follow her, committing herself to move to her left.

3 With the defender committed, the attacker stops moving to her right and pushes off to her left.

CHANGES OF PACE AND DIRECTION

A sudden change of direction, speed or both can be important in getting free of a marker. A player can fake a move in one direction (see above), or pivot quickly on one foot to move away in a different direction. Changes of running speed can also outwit defenders (see page 19, top). If you find a change of speed or direction has not got you free from an opponent, try another move to get into space.

4 The attacker is now in space, while the defender is left behind, having committed herself in the wrong direction.

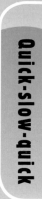

1 Here, an attacker in blue is using a change of pace to get free from a marker in red. She runs forwards quickly, closely followed by the marker, before slowing rapidly.

2 The defender also slows down. However, the attacker has stayed on the balls of her feet and is ready to sprint forwards again, giving the defender little time to react.

3 With a rapid change of pace, the attacker sprints forwards again, leaving the defender behind. The attacker sticks her hand out to signal to a team-mate that she is ready to receive a pass.

1 Here, the attacker in blue runs towards her team-mate who has the ball. The defender in red follows this run, marking the attacker closely.

2 The attacker checks her forwards run and quickly runs backwards. The defender cannot follow this change of direction quickly enough.

3 With the attacker free from her marker, her team-mate launches a shoulder pass over the defender.

HELPING OUT

Getting free means not just getting into space but getting into a place on the court where your team-mate with the ball can reach you with a pass. Try not to get too far away from your team-mate to receive a pass. As players attack, they want to move the ball forwards, but, sometimes, they may have to pass backwards or to the side to keep the attack going. Stay alert to possible passing options and look to help out a team-mate in trouble by offering them an easy passing chance.

As with any skill, getting free from a defender can be practised. Here, two players are taking it in turns to get free from each other.

19

ATTACKING

Only four players in a team (Centre, Wing Attack, Goal Attack and Goal Shooter) are allowed in the attacking third of the court. Their aim is to work together to pass, or feed, the ball into the shooting circle and create a chance to score.

PASSING PLAYS

There are many different passing moves and plays that can be used by netball teams to get the ball into a scoring position. These are practised in training over and over again so that everyone in the team knows exactly what they have to do. One of the simplest moves is the one-two pass. This sees a player pass the ball, then sprint past a defender to receive a return pass. Whichever attacker has the ball, she must select the right pass type and, as soon as the pass is made, quickly get into a good position in space to receive another pass and continue the attack.

One-two

1 Here, the Goal Attack in blue plays a short pass to her team-mate, over the head of the defender in red.

2 As soon as she has made the pass, the Goal Attack sprints to her left.

3 The defender, who was watching the pass, has been caught off-guard and left behind, and the Goal Attack now finds herself free of her marker.

4 Now that she is in space, the Goal Attack can receive a return pass from her team-mate and the attack can continue.

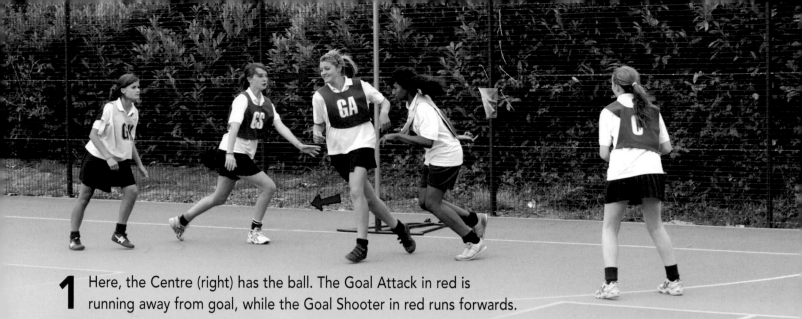

1 Here, the Centre (right) has the ball. The Goal Attack in red is running away from goal, while the Goal Shooter in red runs forwards.

2 The defender marking the Goal Attack has run forwards as well, leaving a space for the Goal Shooter to run into.

3 With the Goal Shooter now in space, she is in a good position to receive a pass from the Centre outside the shooting circle.

4 Once the Goal Shooter has received the pass, she can turn and take a shot at goal.

USING THE COURT

Players should always think about how they will use any spaces around the court. In the excitement of a netball match, it can be easy to get drawn towards the action, and players can end up bunched around a ball. However, this can leave large areas of space. Players can run into space to receive a pass or draw a defender away from a position, freeing up that space for another attacker to run into (see above).

Here, the Goal Attack in red has spotted space farther down the court. She has thrown a long pass down the court for her team-mates to run onto, being careful not to break the over-a-third rule.

Side pass

Sometimes, a pass towards the goal is not the best. Here (below), the attacker in blue does not have a clear pass into the shooting circle. Instead, she passes to a team-mate standing to one side to continue the attack.

DEFENDING

A team defends when it does not have possession of the ball. The priority for a defending team is to stop the opposition team from moving the ball up the court and into a scoring position.

MARKING UP

In most junior games, teams defend using player-to-player marking. Defenders get close to opponents without bumping, barging or pushing them and then stick with them as they move about the court. The aim is to deny opponents the space and time to make an easy catch or pass. A well-marked attacker is unlikely to receive a pass. In effect, you as the defender have taken the attacker out of the game. Being a marker is a constant job, as the attacker may make a sudden sprint or break to try to get free. Stay on the balls of your feet with your legs apart and knees slightly bent, so that you are ready to move in any direction to keep up with your opponent.

Marking involves staying close to your opponent and watching out for sudden changes of pace or direction.

Getting in position

1 The Goal Attack in red has just received a pass. The Goalkeeper who was marking her is moving forwards into a defending position.

2 The Goalkeeper must stay at least 0.9 metres (3 feet) away from the Goal Attack's landing foot, otherwise she will give away a penalty pass.

3 The Goalkeeper stands on tiptoes to get as much height as possible and holds her arms out to block the likely path of a pass.

Intercepting

1 Here, the defending player in red has spotted a loose pass between the two attacking players wearing blue.

DEFENDING ON THE BALL

When the player you are marking receives the ball, your aim is to stop a pass. Keep watching the player and the ball and move to cover your opponent if she pivots and turns round. Watch out for attempts by your opponent to trick and unbalance you with a pretend pass in one direction, and try to stay balanced at all times. You cannot touch the ball while it is in your opponent's hands, but once the ball is released you can jump up or lunge to the side to intercept or block the pass.

2 The defending player quickly runs in front of the receiving attacker to try to intercept the pass.

3 By jumping high, the defending player has successfully caught the ball, intercepting the pass and securing possession for her own team.

Keeping an eye on both the ball and the opponent you are marking may seem a tall order, but defenders seek to do both. This can sometimes allow them to rush in or jump to intercept a poor pass by their opponents.

23

SHOOTING

To win a game, you have to score more points than your opponents. You can do this only with accurate shooting. To shoot, a Goal Attack or Goal Shooter must be inside the shooting circle. If another player puts the ball through the hoop, the goal does not count.

1 At the start of the shooting movement, the Goal Shooter squats slightly by flexing both of her knees.

2 To shoot the ball towards the hoop, the Goal Shooter straightens her legs and arms at the same time, releasing the ball at the highest point.

SHOOTING TECHNIQUE

Every experienced netball player may have a slightly different shooting technique, but there are some points that apply to nearly all methods of shooting. As soon as you get the ball, turn to face the goal, focus your eyes on the back of the hoop and line up your body. Stand with your feet slightly apart and your weight evenly balanced. The shooting action does not start from the arms. It starts from the legs flexing and then straightening. This action is carried through the body and ends with the ball released from the fingertips and the arms following through in the direction of the shot.

3 The Goal Shooter keeps her back straight throughout the shot and she follows through with her arms towards the hoop to ensure an accurate shot.

SHOOTING PRACTICE

Just like a player passing the ball, a shooter has just three seconds to shoot, so lining up and taking a shot has to be done quickly and under pressure. Concentrate on your technique and practise by repeating the exact same shooting action over and over again. Get your coach to watch you and suggest improvements. You should also set yourself targets when practising, such as scoring a certain number of shots out of ten from one position in the shooting circle before moving on to shoot from a different place in the circle. As you progress, practise your shooting with a team-mate acting as an opponent, defending in front of you.

These players are practising their shooting skills. They are taking shots from all parts of the shooting circle as you never know for certain where you will receive a pass.

Getting a good grip

When taking a shot, the ball is balanced on one hand and raised above the head as high as the attacker can manage. This keeps it out of the reach of a guarding defender. The other hand can be used to hold the ball steady. The shooter's focus should be on the hoop all the time – any break in concentration could lead to a wayward shot.

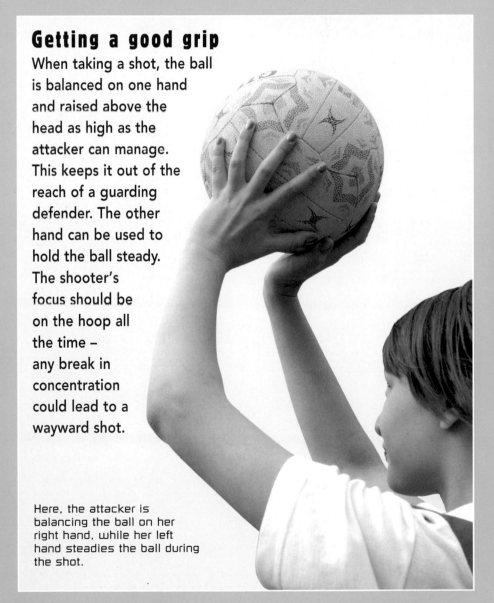

Here, the attacker is balancing the ball on her right hand, while her left hand steadies the ball during the shot.

Here, the Goal Shooter has caught the ball very close to the foot of the post and a Goalkeeper has stepped into a defensive position. To get a better angle for the shot, the Goal Shooter has decided to take a step back. She must keep her landing foot off the ground throughout the shot.

25

THE SHOOTING CIRCLE

Inside the shooting circle is where netball games are won or lost. The two pairs of team-mates who play in and around the circle work closely together to either make or prevent scoring opportunities.

IN ATTACK

The Goal Shooter and Goal Attack seek out space in the shooting circle and time their runs to meet passes from attacking team-mates. The pair can decide to stay deep in the back half of the attacking third, or rove outside of the circle, helping out with attacking moves. The pair can decide who takes the lead to take a pass from outside the circle from the Wing Attack or Centre. Once the ball is inside the shooting circle, there are still decisions to be made. A player can decide to shoot or, if she is not in a good shooting position, she can decide to pass the ball to her team-mate who may be standing in a better position.

The Goal Attack in blue has just received a pass inside the shooting circle. She now has the choice to either pass to the Goal Shooter, who might have a clearer shot at the goal, or to take a shot herself.

1 With two attackers and two defenders, the shooting circle can be a very crowded place. Making space for a shooting chance will make scoring easier.

2 The two attackers in red have pushed the defenders back towards the post, leaving plenty of space out towards the front of the circle.

3 The two attackers quickly turn and step away from their markers, giving the Centre the option of passing to either of them.

4 In this case, the Centre has passed to the Goal Shooter, who has caught the ball in space.

IN DEFENCE

The defending players try to prevent the ball being thrown into the shooting circle. The Goalkeeper tends to mark the Goal Shooter closely while the Goal Defence marks the Goal Attack. The defenders shadow the attackers as they move about the attacking third, without blocking or obstructing them. When an opponent does get the ball inside the circle, the marking defender gets in line between the shooter and the post and takes up a defending position (see page 22). Even after a shot has been made, players will watch the ball in the air and stay alert for potential rebounds off the post or the hoop.

A rebound off the hoop or a poor shot or pass into the shooting circle will see players from both teams competing to grab the ball.

NETBALL TACTICS

Tactics are different moves and ways of playing netball that are decided on by a coach and the team. Different tactics are practised frequently in training so that every member of the team knows what they have to do.

PRACTISING MOVES

Netball training involves exercises to improve speed and fitness levels and to improve your passing, catching, moving, defending and shooting skills. It also gives the players and coach a chance to practise different tactics to use during the game. Defending tactics include double-teaming an opposing player (see below) or exploiting weak opposition passers on a team by pressurising them with more than one defender. The pressurised player may hold onto the ball for more than three seconds and give away a free pass. Attacking tactics include holding space (see page 29) or varying the moves used for centre pass restarts.

(see page 29)

This team is practising fast passing and running moves.

Here, two defenders in blue are double-teaming the Goal Attack. This is when two defenders mark an attacker closely.

Flooding the defence

If a team is behind with not much time left in the game, it may perform a tactic called flooding. Four or five defenders (shown here wearing red) surge into the part of the court where the ball is, congesting the area and making it hard to pass the ball.

1 The Goal Attack in red is running towards the Centre, while the Goal Shooter steps to her right.

2 By stepping to her right and standing still, the Goal Shooter is holding that space in the shooting circle and blocking the defender in blue from running with the Goal Attack.

Holding space

3 With the defender blocked, the Goal Attack is now free from her marker and in space to receive a pass from the Centre. She can now turn and take a shot at the goal.

CENTRE PASS TACTICS

During a game, your team will take many centre passes. Teams may vary these restarts. For example, players can overload one side of the court leaving plenty of space on the other side of the court for a team-mate to run into. A team can also use a split strategy where the Wing Attack sprints to one side of the passer and the Goal Attack to the other. Another tactic is for the Wing Attack and Goal Attack to sprint towards the passer and then turn back towards the shooting circle, leaving space in the middle third for the Wing Defence or Goal Defence to rush into.

One simple way to change tactics is to change players. Coaches can substitute players at any time.

Glossary

attacking third The third of the court that contains the shooting circle, inside which a team's Goal Shooter and Goal Attack play.

backlines The lines at each end of the court.

centre pass A pass made by a team's Centre from the centre circle. Centre passes are used to start a game of netball and to restart the game after a goal has been scored.

double-teaming When two members of the defending team both mark the same opponent.

feed A precise pass into the shooting circle.

free pass A pass awarded to one team when the other team has broken a rule of the game, such as stepping, being offside or catching the ball, dropping it and catching it again.

held ball When a player in control of the ball holds onto it for more than three seconds.

interception When a player catches the ball from a pass that was meant for an opponent.

marking A defending technique where a player stays close to an opponent, denying them the time and space to receive the ball or make a pass.

offside An offence when a player with or without the ball leaves the areas of the court that they are allowed in.

overhead pass A two-handed pass made by throwing the ball over the head.

pivoting When a player keeps one foot in the same place but swivels round, taking steps with the other foot to change the direction they are facing.

quarters The four playing periods, each 15 minutes long, into which a game of netball is divided.

rebound When the ball bounces off either the hoop or the goal post and stays in play after a failed shot.

shooting circle The semi-circle with a radius of 4.9 metres (16 feet) which surrounds the goal post and inside which players can attempt a shot at goal.

shoulder pass A strong, fast pass, used over long distances and thrown from the shoulder.

stepping An offence when a player with the ball takes too many steps without releasing it.

throw-in A throw awarded to the team who did not touch the ball last before it left the court.

toss-up A way of restarting play after a player from each team breaks a rule at the same time or when two players catch the ball at the same time.

transverse lines The two lines that run across the court from sideline to sideline and divide the court into thirds.

umpires The two officials who run and control a game of netball.

Diet and nutrition

A healthy diet contains plenty of fresh fruit and vegetables, as well as wholewheat pasta and rice that contain lots of carbohydrates, and only small amounts of sugary or fatty foods. Proteins are important in building muscle strength and they can be found in lean fish and meat as well as pulses, such as beans and chickpeas.

Try to make sure that you eat a meal at least two hours before playing. If you eat closer to game time, you are likely to feel sluggish. If you are taking part in a netball tournament with a number of games throughout the day, pack some healthy snacks, such as cereal bars, yoghurt and fresh fruit to help improve your energy levels between matches.

Netball is a high-energy sport and in warm ups, training and in matches you can lose a lot of body fluids through sweat, especially on warm days. Always carry a water bottle containing water, juice or fruit squash in your sports bag. Take small sips regularly to keep the fluids in your body topped up.

http://www.internationalnetball.com/netball_nutrition.html
The international netball website has this handy webpage on diet and nutrition.

Resources

www.ucl.ac.uk/~uczcw11/netorgs.htm
Countries that have a national netball team usually have an organisation that runs the sport such as England Netball, Netball Australia or the Welsh Netball Association. At the top of the sport is the International Federation of Netball Associations (IFNA), which runs the sport globally. This website lists local and national netball organisations in different countries.

www.netball.org/
The homepage of the International Netball Federation, which includes details of world rankings and much more besides.

www.live.englandnetball.co.uk/
England Netball's website contains features, news and results.

www.netball.asn.au/
Netball Australia's website includes biographies of star players, photos and videos.

www.netballnz.co.nz/
The official website of New Zealand netball has rules, tips and team profile sections.

www.bbc.co.uk/schools/gcsebitesize/pe/video/netball/
Nine short but handy videos on different netball skills can be found on this webpage.

www.anz-championship.com/
The latest news, results and stories from the ANZ Championship can be found here.

INDEX

Out to Sea

HELEN KELLOCK